Squirrels

Furry Scurriers

by Becky Olien

Consultant:
Peg Halloran, Ph.D.
Associate Professor of Biology
United States Air Force Academy, Colorado

Bridgestone Books
an imprint of Capstone Press
Mankato, Minnesota

Bridgestone Books are published by Capstone Press
151 Good Counsel Drive, P.O. Box 669, Mankato, Minnesota 56002
http://www.capstone-press.com

Library of Congress Cataloging-in-Publication Data
Olien, Rebecca.
    Squirrels : furry scurriers/by Becky Olien.
    p. cm.—(The wild world of animals)
    Includes bibliographical references (p. 24) and index.
    Summary: Describes the physical characteristics, behavior, food, predators, and
habitat of squirrels, as well as their relationship with people.
    ISBN 0-7368-1139-7
    1. Squirrels—Juvenile literature. [1. Squirrels.] I. Title. II. Series.
QL737.R68 O38 2002
599.36—dc21   2001004198

Editorial Credits
Megan Schoeneberger, editor; Karen Risch, product planning editor; Linda Clavel,
    designer and illustrator; Heidi Schoof, photo researcher

Photo Credits
Craig Brandt, 8
Jack Dermid/Visuals Unlimited, cover
Jack Macfarlane, 12
Joe McDonald, 6, 20
Joe McDonald/Visuals Unlimited, 18
John Gerlach/TOM STACK & ASSOCIATES, 16
PhotoDisc, Inc., 1, (texture) cover, 2, 3, 6, 8, 10, 12, 18, 22, 23, 24
Robert McCaw, 10
S. Maslowski/Visuals Unlimited, 14
Tom & Pat Leeson, 4

1 2 3 4 5 6 07 06 05 04 03 02

Table of Contents

kaibab squirrel

tail

claws

toes

Squirrels

Squirrels can have brown, red, or gray fur. Ground squirrels often have light spots. Most squirrels have long, furry tails. They have two large black eyes. Squirrels have short legs. They have sharp claws and toes that bend to help them climb.

Squirrels' front teeth keep growing. They can grow 6 inches (15 centimeters) each year. But the teeth do not get too long because gnawing wears them down.

Columbian ground squirrel

Squirrels Are Mammals

Squirrels are warm-blooded. They have a backbone and fur like other mammals. Female mammals give birth to live young. The young drink milk from their mothers. Squirrels belong to the rodent family. Rodents use their long front teeth to gnaw.

gnaw
to bite or chew

The smallest squirrel is the African Pygmy. It is only about 2.5 inches (6 centimeters) long.

South African ground squirrel

A Squirrel's Habitat

Squirrels live in habitats around the world. Tree squirrels make their homes in trees. Pine squirrels live in pine forests. Gray squirrels can live in forests or cities. Ground squirrels dig burrows in the ground. Some ground squirrels live in deserts.

habitat
the place where
an animal lives

Douglas squirrels and red squirrels sometimes are called pine squirrels. They get their name because they gather pinecones into small hills.

Douglas squirrel

What Do Squirrels Eat?

Squirrels eat seeds and berries. They eat pinecones and nuts from trees. Squirrels also eat insects and bird eggs. Most tree squirrels store food to eat when other food becomes hard to find. Ground squirrels do not store food for winter. They hibernate in their burrows.

hibernate
to spend the winter
in a deep sleep

golden mantle ground squirrel

Predators

Squirrels have many predators. Foxes and raccoons eat squirrels. Hawks and owls also eat squirrels. Tree squirrels leap from tree to tree to escape predators. Ground squirrels run down into their burrows. Some squirrels make a loud noise to warn other squirrels of danger.

predator
an animal that hunts and eats other animals

gray squirrel and pups

Mating and Birth

Male squirrels chase female squirrels before mating. Females give birth about one month after mating. They have three to five pups. Pups are young squirrels. They are born without fur. They cannot hear or see. Pups grow quickly. They have soft fur in a few weeks.

red squirrel

Making a Home

Squirrels need a home away from weather and predators. Females need a place to give birth. Ground squirrels live in burrows. Many tree squirrels build dens in tree holes. Some squirrels make large nests called dreys. They use moss or pine needles to keep their nests warm.

drey

a nest built in the tops of trees by some squirrels

southern flying squirrel

FUN FACTS

Flying squirrels can glide up to 200 feet (61 meters) between trees.

Daring Scurriers

Squirrels often scurry. They run quickly and easily. Tree squirrels use their tails to balance on thin branches. Flying squirrels have folds of skin between their front and back legs. They stretch their legs to glide between trees.

glide
to move smoothly and easily through the air

gray squirrel

Squirrels and People

People have different feelings about squirrels. Some people think squirrels are pests. Squirrels eat garden plants and seeds from bird feeders. But many people enjoy watching squirrels. People sometimes try to help squirrels at rehabilitation centers.

rehabilitation center
a place where sick or hurt animals get treated

Hands On: Gliding

Flying squirrels have a fold of skin between their front and back legs. They do not really fly. They glide from tree to tree. Try this experiment to see how gliding works.

What You Need

Pencil
Sheet of paper
Tape

What You Do

1. Hold the pencil in front of you. Let go and watch it drop to the ground.
2. Lay out the sheet of paper horizontally. Place the pencil in the middle of the paper.
3. Fasten the pencil in place with two or three pieces of tape.
4. Hold the paper in front of you, pencil side down. Let go and watch how the pencil glides to the ground.

The paper acts like the folds of skin between a flying squirrel's legs. The paper slows the fall of the pencil. The flying squirrel uses its extra skin to glide from tree to tree.

Words to Know

den (DEN)—the place where a wild animal lives; many squirrels build dens in tree holes.

drey (DRAY)—a nest built in the tops of trees by some squirrels

habitat (HAB-uh-tat)—the place where an animal lives

mate (MATE)—to join together to produce young

rehabilitation center (ree-huh-bil-uh-TAY-shun SEN-tur)—a place where sick or hurt animals get treated; the animals are freed once they are able to live on their own.

rodent (ROHD-uhnt)—a mammal with long front teeth used for gnawing; squirrels, beavers, and mice are rodents.

warm-blooded (warm-BLUHD-id)—having a body temperature that stays the same

Read More

Fowler, Allan. *Squirrels and Chipmunks.* Rookie Read-About Science. New York: Children's Press, 1997.

Miller, Sara Swan. *Rodents: From Mice to Muskrats.* Animals in Order. New York: Franklin Watts, 1998.

Internet Sites

Enchanted Learning—Flying Squirrel
http://www.enchantedlearning.com/subjects/ mammals/rodent/flyingsquirrelprintout.shtml

The Squirrel Almanac
http://spot.colorado.edu/~halloran/sqrl.html

Squirrel Wildlife Rehabilitation
http://www.squirrel-rehab.org

Index